Our De**▯**

Journey

A collection of heartfelt and emotional poems
about one family's journey including messages
of hope and advice for those on the same
journey

By

Patrick J McTaggart

Poems in Celebration of Mum and Dad
For the love they have always shown us and
the lives they have given us.

ISBN: 9798357433688

Contents

Introduction

My Dad, also called Pat, was diagnosed with dementia several years ago. Over the last couple of years my Mum's health has deteriorated from a physical perspective and she now has no mobility and suffers from a deal of pain. I live with my parents and am the main carer for them both, having retired early from my job in finance. The journey we are on since Dad was diagnosed with dementia is very much a family affair for Dad, my Mum Margaret, my sister Donna and my brother Steven.

As a carer for Dad I know how difficult both physically and emotionally dementia can be for both the person who has it and close family particularly those who are carers day to day. Relationships can be strained but also strengthened and I truly believe that love conquers all. Despite the pain, the dementia journey can still provide gifts of memories that will last forever.

It is true to say that no one person's dementia journey is exactly the same as anyone else's and it is also true to say that family members who are carers can go through moments of emotional despair when nothing they try to do seems to work.

Very often family carers are forced to learn as they go. My nature in times such as these leads me to dip into books by professionals with experience and knowledge of dementia to see if I can find anything to help me. Sometimes I do and sometimes I don't. Often books can be quite long and time to research on the other hand very short. It was only by chance that I saw on-line some quotes about dementia and these really hit the mark with me. They were succinct and seemed to understand what I was going through. Researching these a bit further I found that many quotes by people who either had dementia or experience of it with a family member had a clarity at both an emotional level and also in terms of giving much needed advice. They were also very easy to read often providing simple lessons from short poems, quotes or songs.

Having never written a poem in my life before suddenly I started writing poems, the first time being in the middle of the night. I found that they helped me by putting down on paper how I was feeling including my emotions and helped me better reflect on and better understand certain situations. Being a carer I find to be a constant process of learning and trying to do things better.

Over time as I wrote more poems, usually early in the morning, I started to think that perhaps some of the things I learned from our dementia journey may be of some small help to others on the same journey or who are about to start it. Poetry seemed to me to be a good way to provide it with fairly short poems often with a simple message.

Much of the advice I have picked up over the years I wish I had received much earlier in the journey. This book is essentially a book of poems which are heartfelt and some of which were very emotional for me writing them, which I hope you will enjoy and empathise with. At the same time I hope that this book will be an easy read and may help others avoid some of the pain and emotional stresses I know I suffered. I do hope there are one or two nuggets in the book that will be helpful to you at some stage of your journey.

In terms of the poems in this collection therefore, I would describe them as:

Poems for me
Poems for you
Poems about the dementia journey our family is going through
Poems with our feelings
Poems with our thoughts
Poems with reflections on the dementia bigger picture too

I should also add that I will receive no payment for any time or effort in writing the book and that all my royalties from the sales of this book will go to Alzheimers Research UK, the world's largest dedicated dementia research charity, in the hope that it will go some way to helping find a cure which I am sure is the common wish of us all.

The final section of this book invites you to write a poem both for your own benefit but also to raise additional funds to support dementia charities. I hope you will give it a go.

Testimonials

"I know well that families coping with dementia find useful insights, tips, acknowledgement, and empathy in a myriad of forms. For those who embrace the soothing, probing wisdom of poetry, we now have Pat McTaggart's *Our Dementia Journey*. 'Everyone has a poem in them,' Pat writes. This parental tribute is a fount of affirmation for those of us touched by Alzheimer's--and may even inspire you to pen your own."

"A wonderful tribute and aid."

Paula Spencer Scott, Award-winning journalist and author *of Surviving Alzheimer's: Practical Tips and Soul-Saving Wisdom for Caregivers*

"This collection of poems that Pat has written is both touching and uplifting. It shows the heartache and the love present in his family's dementia journey.

We're so grateful to Pat for supporting Alzheimer's Research UK. Fantastic fundraising efforts like this collection of poems will help us to make life-changing research breakthroughs for people with dementia."

Bernie Carranza, Regional Fundraising Officer at Alzheimer's Research UK

Alzheimers Research UK

Alzheimer's Research UK is the UK's leading dementia research charity, dedicated to causes, diagnosis, prevention, treatment and cure. Backed by passionate scientists and supporters, it is challenging the way people think about dementia, uniting the big thinkers in the field and funding the innovative science that will deliver a cure.
It is working across four key areas of action.

- Understand the diseases that cause dementia.

- Diagnose people earlier and more accurately.

- Reduce risk, backed by the latest evidence.

- Treat dementia effectively.

It funds a broad range of research projects to understand dementia and drive us towards better diagnosis, preventions and treatments.
It has invested in over 1000 projects across all forms of dementia since 1998. It has funded thousands of dementia researchers based in more than 100 institutions in the UK and around the world.

Through these important strands of work, it is bringing about breakthroughs that will change lives.
Its vision is a world where people are free from the fear, harm and heartbreak of dementia.

Its mission is to bring about the first life-changing dementia treatment by 2025.

If you would like to know more about Alzheimers Research UK and the work it does please visit their website:

www.alzheimersresearchuk.org

In aid of

Alzheimer's Research UK

Mum and Dad

This collection of poems is in many ways a celebration of Mum and Dad and our love for them both as well as the journey we are on. The first two poems reflect this.

The Dementia Train

Dad has just boarded the Dementia train
With seats for all the family to share in the pain
More and more carriages are added each day
To make room for the many going this way
The journey may be long and of many stages
But without any stations to make any changes
Most people on board count many years one and all
But some early on-boarders have also heard the call
The windows reflect memories personal and shared
Of the people in the seats with whom they are paired
The music and singing is a joy to behold
With singers and dancers stepping forward so bold
As the journey progresses the windows mist up
Like the connections in the brain that sadly dry up
The memories grow foggy
The journey more rocky
Silence takes over from singing
Loving and caring, caring and loving, loving becomes
caring
Holding hands and hugs till journey's end
Never left to ride alone or in need of a friend

Mum and Dad

It's difficult now Mum
Struggling so hard to walk, even with sticks and wheels
to hold
Legs and feet refusing to do as they are told
Trapped inside, confined to a chair
Not able to go out, it just doesn't seem fair

It's difficult now Dad
Since Dementia came calling some time ago
Memories have faded and names of loved ones also
Trapped inside your mind, confined by dementia to
remain there
Not always able to get the right words out, it just
doesn't seem fair

It's difficult now Mum
Dad forever tells you he loves you and holds on to your
hand
But a lot of the time he doesn't recognise you and can't
understand

It's difficult now Dad
Mum can't go on long walks with you and hold on to
your arm
You don't know why and often ask how it would do
any harm

One sharp mind and one strong body shared between two
Forever a partnership with love always shining through

It's difficult now Mum and for you too Dad
But please oh please don't give up
We all care too much to see you give up
Your family are always here with you to comfort and to cheer both of you
A family united through love that will always see us through

Dementia – Dad's Perspective

When a family member writes about their loved one's dementia, whether it is poetry or anything else, I think it is important that they sometimes imagine themselves in the shoes of the person with dementia. The poems in this section therefore attempt to focus and think about the journey we are on from Dad's perspective.

Forget Me Not

I noticed I had started to forget things more than just
the norm
I guessed it might be dementia and my guess was more
than just warm

It's unclear the exact road that I will now follow
But there are I'm afraid some things that I do know
My personality may change in some ways and
challenging behaviours come to the fore
And perhaps worse still, for me at least, I will start to
forget things, more and more and more

I already forget where I have left things and forget
names that I should know
I regularly repeat what I have just said which I am sure
you already know
I recently went for a long walk in the park
And embarrassingly had trouble finding my way back

As time goes on I will forget things even more than
now
There may be no rhyme nor reason to what or who or
how
I may forget the place I call my home
I may forget where the different rooms are inside my
home

I may forget what happened yesterday
I may forget what day it is today or even whether it is
night or day
Worst of all I fear that I may forget the names of loved
ones, or worse still who they are
I hope for you Dear Family it doesn't go that far

Behind the challenging behaviours and forgetfulness
I want you to know that I will still be me nonetheless
I may be harder to find, as time goes on
But I will be in there still, I will not be gone
I pray therefore that however much I do forget, and
stop it I cannot
I ask you one thing Dear Loved Ones, please forget me
not

How must it feel?

How must it feel to not know where you are?
How must it feel to not know who people are?
How must it feel to wake up not knowing each day?
How must it feel when you don't see properly?
How must it feel to want always to go home?
How must it feel when you are all alone?
How must it feel when names you forget?
How must it feel when you can't find the toilet?
How must it feel when you can't understand?
How must it feel when you can't stand?
How must it feel when you wake up in the dark?
How must it feel when you can't find your way back
from the park?
How must it feel to not know where you should be?
How must it feel to not know what you should do?
How must it feel?

Hold on to me

When I can't find my way, hold on to me
When I am lost, hold on to me
When we are in crowds, hold on to me
When we are alone, hold on to me
When I am unsteady on my feet, hold on to me
When I just need a seat, hold on to me
When I forget who people are, hold on to me
When I forget who you are, hold on to me
When I can't see things properly, hold on to me
When I get things wrong, hold on to me
When I get angry and shout, hold on to me
When I forget what it's all about, hold on to me
When it's time to go to bed, hold on to me
When it's time to get up, hold on to me
When I am scared, hold on to me
Forever and always Dear Dad, I'll hold on to you
But one thing I ask please Dear Lord, anchor me.

Dementia – My Perspective

The poems in this section are mainly written in terms of my perspective on the journey we are on. It includes both my thoughts and feelings on Dad's dementia and how it has affected Dad as well as the family. It covers our relationship, Dad's behaviours, what makes him happy and what upsets him. It includes poems on things that go well and things that do not.

What I didn't know

When Dad was diagnosed with dementia a good few
years ago
There was a great deal about dementia that I did not
know
I knew that dementia would steal away memory
Not all at once but gradually
Dad had already started to repeat himself that I did
know
Names and places and short term memory I knew
would go
And in the worst case names and knowledge of loved
ones also
Last to go being memories and thoughts from long ago

I didn't know there were many different types of
dementia
with Alzheimers to the fore
But also Vascular, Young Onset, Dementia with Lewy
bodies, and even more

I didn't know the challenging behaviours dementia can
bring
These include shadowing, hoarding, pacing, checking
and sometimes accusing
A constant desire to go home when actually already
there can be especially challenging

As well as the time of day known as sundowning

I didn't know the impact dementia can have on vision
Not something that can always be fixed by a visit to an
optician
Just as scary for the person is a mirror and its reflection

For someone living with dementia, I didn't know quite
how calming music can be
Singing and music often holds the key to the magic of
the mind you see

I didn't know the stages that a person with dementia
can go through
Or that everyone is unique and each person's journey
can vary, it is true
I didn't know how dealing first with emotion would be
to the fore
And logic would matter little any more

I didn't know that some tablets can slow dementia's
progress
But no treatment to cure it or even make it regress

I didn't know the impact lifestyle can have on the risk
of getting dementia
With heart health, smoking and drinking factors to
consider
Along with diet, brain health and keeping socially
active as well as just getting older

I didn't know where to turn to for help, I wasn't
advised, strangely

Doctors and specialists importantly
But charities and other organisations equally

As I said at the start there was lots about dementia that
I didn't know
Even today it is still the case I have to confess this is so
Though I know much more than I did at the start I am
learning every day
As the saying goes every day is very much a school day
If you have been diagnosed with dementia or are caring
for someone who has
Hopefully the words above will give some direction to
things to find out or to ask
This will hopefully prepare you better and take some
stress away
After that all you can do is take things day by day

Early Signs

Reflecting one day on points to ponder
Some things, like those below, did give us cause to
wonder

One year we went on holiday to Troon, by the sea
Each evening at dinner Dad said to Mum and to me
We've been here before I remember it well
Pointing out the different features that he could tell
Mum and I both knew we had never been to Troon
before
But convincing Dad of this became a nigh impossible
chore
Each evening Dad repeated the same conversation to
Mum and to me
An early sign of dementia that we now see

In autumn time the leaves fall from the trees
Landing in our garden, replacing the summer flowers
and the bees
In the land behind there are many trees and lots and
lots of leaves do fall
For Dad that was like a distant call
We had to go out and sweep up leaves everywhere
Making sure that all paths they were clear
In itself this was fine
But rain hail or shine

It became more obsessive over time
Even when the wind was blowing hard
Dad wanted to go out and clear the backyard
Convincing Dad otherwise was not to be
Neither by Mum or by me
An early sign of dementia that we now see

The Nightshift

Dad has dementia and sometimes I wonder
How much it was caused by poor quality slumber
For many years my Dad had to go to work at night
Having to sleep during the day when it was light
On days off it would change to sleeping at night
This is a combination not easy to get right

Scientists tell us Alzheimers can be caused by amyloid
building up in the brain
But with deep sleep each night then from the brain it
can drain
Amyloid protein is nasty you can tell
As it builds up it damages many a brain cell

I know that my Dad found it difficult to sleep
The hours they were few and the quality not deep
You can see why I think Nightshift is to blame
And why like a thief in the night dementia came

Love conquers all

What do you do if your Dad argues with the mirror?
What do you do if your Dad asks 20 times if you want
some tea?
What do you do if your Dad visits the smallest room
again and again and again?
What do you do if your Dad forgets your name?
What do you do if your Dad can't sleep at night?
What do you do if your Dad carries his cup around
with him and won't let you wash it?
What do you do if your Dad says angrily that his
money has been stolen?
What do you do if your Dad asks over and over for you
to take him home when he is at home?
You Love him.

What is love?

Love is when your Dad continually asks if you want some tea
Love is when your Dad always offers you some of his meal before he will eat it
Love is when your Dad asks you many times a day if you are ok
Love is when your Dad always wants to know where you are
Love is when your Dad is waiting at the door on you coming home from work
Love is when your Dad always thanks you for the smallest gesture of kindness
Love is when your Dad says thank you son with a smile when you tuck him up in bed every night

Where is Home?

I want to go home -
Home is where my wife is
Home is where the family is
Home is where the children are
Home is a place
Home is a person
Home is my house
Home is where I live
Home is where my Mum and Dad are
Home is where the heart is
Home is a feeling
Home is a memory
Home is warm
Home is sweet
Home is comforting
Home is in the past
Home is in the present
-    Home is where we will all be one day Dad

I want to go home

Dad wants to go home – but I thought it was here.
I want to go home – you are home Dad
So can you take me home son please,
I have a wife and a family that will be worried about
me
-   But you are at home Dad, we live here

I need to see my Mum and Dad, so can you help me get
home
-   Would you like some tea Dad

I just want to go home
-   Please don't bang on the door Dad

Let me out I want to go home
-   Would you like to go a run in the car Dad?

And I can go home?
-   Yes, Dad but we will be coming back home to Mum for
    tea later

I just want to go home son
Persistence outruns logic again and again and again

Mirror, Mirror

Mirror mirror on the wall
My Dad is talking to you and he's having a ball
He's laughing and joking with a friend
Is it real or just pretend?

Mirror mirror on the wall
My Dad is talking to you but you're saying nothing at all,
He's getting angry and frustrated you are no longer a friend
Is it real or just pretend?

Sing

Dad is on a mission to get the world to sing
From the shocked old couple crossing the green, wondering
To the head-phoned young man sitting on the park bench, smiling

Since Dementia came calling
Dad's memories have faded, and names may be gone
The key to his mind now is to put the music on

With smiling and laughter aplenty
The singing and dancing is a joy to behold
Who would ever want to put the music on hold

The words to songs both old and new come flooding from Dad
In tune and on key with memory no problem at all
Who's winning now Dementia let me ask you once and for all?

In person or on screen is equally as good
For Family at home and on Facetime when not
Having a song at the ready helps Dad a lot

Travelling or not, there is no excuse, the music must never end

In the car it is essential to have the volume up and the radio or CDs on
From journey's start to journey's end we must all sing along

A little less conversation a lot more singing please
A motto for Dad and one that makes him feel more at ease
A motto also for the world one can only hope please

Who am I?

Some days I have many names.
Son
Patrick – that's the same name as me.
Pat
Paddy
Paderewski
Pa Pa – am I the father now?
Some days I have no name at all because Dad's
memory won't allow it.
Who are you again?

Driving Home

Driving home from work one evening a few years ago
I was just a couple of miles from home when a song
came on the radio
"I'll do the remembering" sang Ashley Campbell in a
song called "Remembering"
A song about remembering as well as forgetting
She had written it for her father the famous actor and
singer Glen
He had been diagnosed and was living with dementia
way back then
The emotion in a song can sometimes make it feel like it
is just for you
Tears flowed from my eyes I have to admit it is very
very true
For my Dad he was at home and he had dementia too

I knew Dad would be waiting as always at the door for
me
Having no doubt asked my Mum just how long I
would be
Dad would wait at the door each night ready to greet
me with a smile
Ask me to come in and sit down here a while
I remembered when I was young I would wait at the
door for Dad

Knowing he would soon be home from work and I was
so glad
I soon arrived home, parked the car and quickly wiped
the tears from me
Went out to meet Dad smiled, gave him a hug and said
let's go in and have our tea

What can I do Dad?

When you can't walk or are struggling to balance
I will hold on to you
When you are lost and don't know where to go
I will show you
When you don't know who different people are
I will tell you
When you don't know who I am
I will remind you
When you forget about things that have past
I will remember for you
When you get up in the middle of the night
I will be there
When you can't sleep and need to get up
I will help you
When you can't see properly
I will be your eyes
When you get angry and shout or forget what it's all
about
I will calm you
When the man in the mirror is upsetting you
I will stop him
When you are feeling frightened and scared
I will hold your hand
When you are in need of a kind word or helping hand
 I will give it

When you need me to put the music on or whistle a
tune
I will do that
When you want us to singalong in the car
I will give it my best
When you want to go for a drive or walk in the park
I will take you
What more can I do for you Dear Dad I ask myself
every day
If there is anything you want please just say

Two Dads and Two Sons

Ever since Dementia came calling, I feel I have two
Dads
I have the Dad I love so much and who always
understood
Who loved and cared and looked after me in every way
he could
Dad and I are similar in oh so many ways, different
chapters of the same book
Alike in personality and temperament and not least in
how we look

Dementia Dad is with us now too an unwanted alter
ego
He can be obstinate, difficult and accusing and often
angry too
And blames me all too often for things that I didn't do
(And doesn't always appreciate the things that I do)

Dementia Dad now has Dementia Son who also looks
just like me
He often doesn't sleep much, and can be impatient and
short tempered too
Just like Dementia Dad he often shouts, and that is
simply not me

Doctors say Dementia, contagious it is not

But Dementia Dad now has Dementia Son and that is contagion is it not

Whether that contagion is long lasting, only time will show
But the Dad I love and the Son that loves him are still very much there I know
They love each other so much and always do the best they can
Even when Dementia does its best to makes things so hard for us all to understand

Dear Dad

Dear Dad – I wish to send this letter to you from me if I may
We both still remember that before dementia came to stay
We never argued or shouted in any way or on any day
I loved you dearly and always will and dementia will never take that away

Dementia came uninvited and threw a net over the whole family
It shakes us about and up and down and challenges us in many a way
Dementia feels contagious in the way it makes us behave
The challenging behaviours come not just from you Dear Dad,
- but from me too in what feels like an unstoppable wave

Whether that contagion is long lasting, only time will show
But the Dad I love and the Son that loves him are still very much here I know

A life in numbers and logic never equipped me for the task
When emotions take over from logic, oh help me Dear Lord I ask

I shout and I argue and I regret the things that I say
Oh please Dear Dad forgive me, and you Dear Lord I pray
I can be tired, lacking in patience, and less tolerant when under pressure in different ways
for these again I say sorry for those many difficult days

Dear Dad you and I are similar in oh so many ways, different chapters of the same book
Alike in personality and temperament and not least in how we look
We are usually kind and calm and not as the challenging behaviours would suggest
Dear Dad you have always been my hero and you will always be the best
So finally Dear Dad I hope that you still know
I love you oh so dearly
And this will always be so.

Damn Disease

Damn you Dementia for what you've done to my Dad
Damn you Dementia for the pain you've made my
Mum suffer and the tears she has shed
Damn you Dementia for the effect you have had on my
family
Damn you Dementia for what you've done to me
Damn you Dementia our love and memories will
outlive you
Damn you Dementia for one day we will have a cure
Damn you Dementia one day you will not get near
Damn you Damn you Damn you Damn you Dementia

Dementia be gone

Dementia we want to find a cure for you
Dementia we want to prevent you
Dementia we want you to forget us
Dementia we want to forget you

Yesterday, Today, Tomorrow

Yesterday was a difficult day
Challenging behaviours lead the way
It didn't seem to matter whatever I'd say

Dad wanted to "go home" wherever that might be
Even though we were at home, Dad doesn't
understand you see
We went for a walk which didn't really help at all
We put music videos on, Dad's favourite songs one and
all
The usual distractions and actions we tried
But nothing seemed to work, I could have cried
Dad argued with mirrors and banged on the door
Everything seemed to annoy him more and more

This went on nearly all day long
Not even a hint of Dad singing a song
Whatever I did seemed to be wrong
My patience and Dad's grew thinner as the day moved
along
We ended up shouting and arguing, which is so wrong

There was some relief in the evening
Music videos on and Dad started singing
We sat together on the couch half singing half sleeping
For us both, after the day, it felt quite calming

A little later it was supper and bed
Dad was very tired
And didn't take long to fall asleep
Which is not always the case on a difficult day, it was
such a relief

Today is very much a different day
Everyone is very tired and flat and lacking in energy
Dad is quite tired and very sleepy
I feel quite guilty and am trying to keep busy
Often it is this way the day after a challenging day
Resting and recharging seems to be the way

Tomorrow will be a different day again
Hopefully a good one when Dad is my "best friend"
Perhaps we'll go out in the afternoon, we'll see
A drive and a walk and stop somewhere for a cup of
tea
Yesterday, today, tomorrow that's three
Days very different which is how it tends to be

Afternoons Out

Often in the afternoon Dad and I would go out in the
car
Sometimes a good run, sometimes not that far
We'd have Dad's favourite music on
So we could both sing along
We'd often stop somewhere for a walk
Or sit in the car and just talk

Some days we'd go to the Kelpies
One of our favourite places
Sea horses rising up so high
Just beside the canal nearby
We'd see the visitors from all over Scotland
Many holding a camera or phone in their hand
And many visitors from overseas
With languages many and varied, so popular are the
Kelpies

On other days we may go and see the Falkirk Wheel
A walk further along the canal or a drive just a little
further still
The world's only rotating boat lift, vessels flying in the
sky
An amazing feat of engineering linking two canals 35m
high
A good place too for hikers alongside Antonine's wall

The tourist board might say "Falkirk has it all"

On other days we might visit the Kingdom, that is Fife
of course
Fife has a lovely coast as well as many a golf course
We like to go for a walk in the lovely park known
locally as the "Glen"
Its proper name is Pittencrieff Park gifted by Andrew
Carnegie to the people of Dunfermline way back when

One thing I didn't mention
The places we choose all have one thing in common
Be it a garden centre, Kelpies, Falkirk Wheel, or the
Glen
There's a nice café nearby, we do like our cup of tea
and scone ye ken

Never walk alone

"You'll never walk alone"[1] goes Dad's favourite song
An anthem to many and for Dad's dementia journey to carry us along
"When you walk through the (dementia) storm"
It would be so hard on your own, and should not be the norm
Surrounded by family makes it easier I'd say
To "Hold your head up high" supporting each other along the way
"Don't be afraid of the dark" days of dementia for they won't stay
"At the end of the storm" when calm is back, at least for today
"There's a golden sky" even if only metaphorically
"And the sweet silver song of the lark" Dad happy and singing again on his journey
Together we must all
"Walk on, through the wind, walk on through the rain, though (our) dreams may be tossed and blown"
Holding hands and hugs till journey's end
Never left to ride alone or in need of a friend
"You'll never walk alone" Dear Dad

References:
"You'll Never Walk Alone" is from the 1945 Rodgers and Hammerstein musical Carousel. A famous cover version was by Gerry and the Pacemakers in 1963.

What will be

My Dad has dementia of which he is unaware
Everyday still he shows us just how much he cares
Dad has faith in all the family, and hope for them all
But the greatest of his emotions, is love for one and all
Dad forever tells us he loves us, and wishes God's
blessings upon us
With loving hugs and kisses, never far from us
Dad's view is 'such is life' and 'what will be will be'
Now isn't that simply a lovely way to be

We are unique

I watched a programme about Dementia on the BBC
It followed the lives of four lovely people with
dementia and each family
They were all very different in how dementia affected
them
And my Dad who has dementia is different yet again
The saying goes that if you have met one person with
dementia
Then you have met one person with dementia
It is true that dementia has certain common traits
But the road that each person will follow is never just
straight
We are all different and unique you see in our own way
And even dementia cannot take that away
Please therefore treat everyone as individuals and with
dignity

Role Reversal

Reflecting on Dad's dementia, one thing that occurs to me
Is the role reversal that has taken place within the family

For Mum, Dad was her rock for more than sixty years
But since dementia came to Dad she has shed a good few tears
Dad forever tells Mum he loves her and holds on to her hand
But a lot of the time he doesn't recognise her and can't understand
Though frail these days and not able to walk
It is Mum's turn now to be Dad's rock

For me and my siblings Mum and Dad always looked after us
With Mum physically frail and Dad with dementia the onus is now upon us
To care for those who cared for us is a great gift and honour to appreciate
Though it may not always feel so it is a hidden gift so great

Dad's dementia brings behavioural challenges that reverse the roles we had

It can sometimes feel that Dad is now the child and I
now need to be the Dad
The need to always know where I am and following me
as I go
The many, many things that Dad has to ask when he
doesn't know
Dad's loving and caring ways and wanting to hold my
hand
Together with behavioural challenges when he doesn't
understand
The need to negotiate on so many things to
accommodate Dad's fears
Can often feel a little bit like he is in his teenage years

As we all grow old
We now all have different roles
Not something, thinking back, anyone would have
foretold
But life is a journey and we must always do the best we
can
Love will see us through, no one left to ride alone or
without a helping hand

Will Dementia Come to Me

My Dad has dementia it is now plain to see
So occasionally I ponder will dementia also come to me
Dementia can be hereditary but mostly it is not
For some risk factors I score low but others I do not

If I get dementia I wonder who would care for me
Would it have to be carers coming in to check on me
daily
I am not married nor have any children so I don't really
know
But I am quite a solitary person and to a home I would
not want to go

When my Dad got dementia he didn't really know
They call it non-awareness and that might suit me also
In terms of what's to come only time will tell for me
So I don't worry about it and as Dad says "what will be
will be"

Dementia – Memories

If you asked anyone who has little experience of dementia about the symptoms of it they would inevitably talk about fading memory. The effects of dementia on memory are significant and so the collection of poems in this section is a reflection on memory in general in relation to dementia as well as some of our family memories.

Memories

Memories often reflect the life that you have lived
Memories for some may be all they have as they grow
old
Memories for others unfortunately fade with time
Memories remembered
Memories forgot
Memories put in a box so they are not
Memories in your mind
Memories written down
Memories in your photos
Memories on-line
Memories on your laptop
Memories on your phone
Wherever they are - share them
Don't keep them all alone
Memories that are shared they do live on
Your legacy and comfort to others after you've gone

Photographs

We have a large cardboard box at home
It is full of the photos we own
Albums they are aplenty
Together with loose photos of which there are many

Some of the photos are in black and white often with
negatives too
Photos of my parents and families growing up – leads
us to guess
Where and what and who's who

Photos of our family growing up are many
Both at home and when we were on holiday
Special events from Christenings to Weddings
Kept in albums, we count our blessings
Photos that trigger memories of what we were doing
just before they were taken
That helps explains some strange expressions
Memories of other senses come flooding back as our
minds run free
The sound of music that was playing or maybe the
smell of the sea
Photos are a picture at a point in time
But remain with us for all time
It's not just the photo on its own
But the joy in the memories they bring back home

More and more photos are taken each day
With mobile phones with us at work rest and play
People share photos on social media and save them on-line
But I do wonder if the value of photos is in decline
Photos of what you are about to eat, or just another selfie or three
Are they really what memories should be?

Remember When...

Remember when I was a boy and lived in Letham
cottages,
My Dad, my two sisters, four brothers and me,
My Mum had sadly passed when I was still wee
My Dad he was a miner and worked underground
Not very tall but strong and well built he was very
proud
We didn't always have a lot but boy we had lots of fun
More stories I could tell, if you have time for another
one

Remember when I was a bit older we crossed the River
Forth
We went to live in Osborne Drive, right at the top of the
hill
I was just fifteen when I started work as an apprentice
gaffer in Paton and Baldwins woolen mill

Remember when I did my National Service, I was in
the army
I was a radio operator in the infantry
We did service in Malta and Cyprus as well as
Germany

Remember when I met my Darling Margaret when she also started work in the mill
We courted and we married and over sixty years later we are happily together still

Remember when, just after Christmas in 1962, our first child was born
It was very cold and there was deep snow on the ground
It was a boy that we named after me and we were so very proud

Remember when, five years later in the summer of 67
The twins were born, a boy and a girl a joy to behold
Number one in the charts at the time we were told
"Those were the days my friend I thought would never end"

Remember when I was younger I really liked to play football
I played inside right for a number of teams and scored many a goal
On Saturday afternoons I'd spent my time at Brockville or East end Park
Watching the two teams that were closest to my heart

Remember when we used to go on family holidays
From caravans on the Fife coast to lodges up north, fun filled every day
Nothing made me happier than being with my family
As time went on we travelled further afield
Spain and Italy had particular appeal

Remember when I retired after 40 years as a gaffer it's
true
We did indeed have a retirement 'do'
When asked what tune I wanted the band to play
One wag he suggested play "I did it my way"
"For that's what he's done for 40 years to this day"

I think that is probably enough memories for one day
I hope that you will treasure them and lock them away
carefully
Though my memory may be fading I trust and know in
my heart
A memory shared with someone you love it will still
live on
My legacy to you my family for long after I am gone

Grandparents

Both Mum and Dad were born in the Kingdom of Fife
A place well known for both its history and its life
My Mum had two sisters as did my Dad
My Mum had three brothers and four brothers my Dad
My Mum's father died when she was so young
In an accident mining deep underground
My Dad's mother died when he was so young
In a hospital in Fife with a fever so strong
Both my Grandads were miners a hard life indeed
Going deep underground to provide for their families'
needs
My Mum's Mum and my Dad's Dad, the grandparents
I knew
Isabella and Ben were both strong people it is certainly
true
Having been widowed so young it was truly so sad
Bringing up large families on their own it was hard
They did all they could bringing up families through
war and strife
Working and caring and loving to give their families
their best life
Both Gran and Grandad have now long since gone
But their memory and character through their stories
and children still live on

Forget

Dementia comes to make us forget
Dementia makes us forget little things just to start with
Dementia makes us forget what we just said
Dementia makes us forget where we are
Dementia makes us forget the way home
Dementia makes us forget where rooms in our home
are
Dementia makes us forget names of loved ones
Dementia makes us forget things that happened
yesterday
Dementia makes us forget things that happened five
minutes ago
Dementia we will find a cure for you
Dementia we will prevent you coming
Then Dementia, we will forget only you

Thief in the night

Dementia comes like a thief in the night
It brings the dark and takes you out of the light
It slowly steals your memories over time and takes
away your past
It steals too your plans for the future you hoped would
last
You must try though to get rid of the dark and create
your own new light
Share your memories with your loved ones that they
may live on and never be out of sight
Make new plans and focus on what you can do still,
that is your future now
Enjoy time with your loved ones and each new day you
can, it is important amidst it all never to forget how

Dementia – Caring

Caring for a loved one who has dementia is not easy. It is new territory for most people and has some challenges unique to the illness that is dementia. You often start from a point of little real knowledge about the illness and it is a case of learning as you go, and also learning to ask for help. You will inevitably get some things wrong and feel all sorts of emotions, sometimes all at the same time. You need to find a way of caring for your loved one while also coping and caring for yourself. We are only human at the end of the day and if we give our best then that is all we can do.

I hope that those on the same journey as me will recognise some of the situations and feelings in these poems and see they are not alone. For those about to go on the journey I hope there are at least some small nuggets within the poems that will help you.

Living Alongside Dementia

Living alongside Dementia can be challenging for all
It is always important therefore to remember things
you must do and others not at all
Don't get impatient when Dad repeats again and again
and again
Don't get frustrated when you have to show Dad the
way over and over again
Don't get upset, when Dad doesn't remember who you
are
Don't complain when Dad doesn't know how to buckle
up when in the car
Don't argue with Dad, logic will never convince him
Don't tell Dad he is wrong you will only upset him
Don't get annoyed when Dad doesn't understand
Don't shout or lose your temper even if you are finding
things difficult to withstand
Do show love and kindness in everything you do
Do imagine yourself in Dad's shoes and think how he
would help you
Do reassure Dad when he seems upset though it may
not be clear why
Do remain calm at all times even if you have to count to
ten and really, really try
Do let your body language be aligned to the calmness
Do make sure you do this otherwise just kind words
are pointless

Do try and see what is upsetting Dad it may be pain
unmentioned
Do look hard to find the reason, that there always is
one should be unquestioned
Do respond to the emotion expressed rather than the
behaviour on the go
Do be kind to yourself as well Dad would want it to be
so
There are may do's and many don'ts to help us all keep
going
Just do your best, and always remember, that's what
Dad is doing.

Vera Says

There are different techniques suggested and VERA[1] is just one
That help to interact with those who have dementia including a loved one
Validate what they are saying is the start
Address the **Emotion** they are feeling is the next important part
Reassuring them has a very important part to play
Then focus thereafter on **Activity**

Paula[2] who knows the Wizards of Alz, has a simple technique which is:
In very basic terms to think "Why this? Try this"
It may sound too simple
But I have found it very useful
It forces you to think what is driving behaviour
Then to try different ways to shift that behaviour
Reassure, Review the cause, Remove any triggers, Redirect is just a part
But it can certainly help if used together with a loving heart

For some things in life putting your head down and fighting through
Can often be very much the right thing for you to do

But in dealing with dementia I suggest it is better "to go round and not go through"
Logic is out the window, and no argument you will win
You may cause further upset and just heighten emotion
Take a step to the side and view it from there
Try a different tact or go a different way, there will be one for sure
You'll get there much quicker if you remain fleet of mind and thought
Even when sadly your loved one is not

References:
1.VERA is a communication framework background developed by Blackhall et al. (2011)
2. Paula refers to Paula Spencer Scott who wrote an excellent book "Surviving Alzheimers" which references the "Wizards of Alz" in the first chapter.

Guilt

Guilt when you can be there
Guilt when you cannot
Guilt when you can do something
Guilt when you cannot
Guilt when you said something that you wish you
hadn't
Guilt when you didn't say something that you wish
you had
Guilt when you did something that you wish you
hadn't
Guilt when you didn't do something that you wish you
had
Guilt during the daytime
Guilt during the night-time
Guilt as a call to action led by your conscience
Guilt as regret and hope when you did not follow your
conscience
Guilt sapping energy from you as a wasted emotion
Guilt in whatever form it comes means it's time to take
positive action
Time to follow your conscience and do what you
should, or
Time to try and make amends in whatever way you
think you still could,
Resolving that next time you will do all that you should

Silent Scream

A silent scream
You know what I mean
Sometimes it is needed, to let off steam
It is loud and it is clear
But no one can hear
And it is nothing to fear
It can help with your sanity
And sometimes bring clarity
Releasing emotions from within
Letting calmness back in
Best done in your private place
Where no-one can see your face
You are after all only part of the human race

Crying room

Caring for loved ones of ages young and old
Is an emotional roller coaster with stories often untold
Moments of great joy, accompany moments of great
pain
For those living this life it can be so hard to explain
Loving and caring, caring and loving, loving becoming
caring
Love and joy, laughter and happiness
Pain and sadness, hopes and regret
Anger and impatience, tiredness and guilt

Churches have their children's crying rooms
Madrid has La Lloreria
The Pope has his "Room of Tears"
Carers too need their private place, somewhere they
can go
To allow the tears to flow sometimes and to let the
emotions go
When they come out of their "crying room" they are
hopefully calmer than before
Ready once more to carry on and put their loved one to
the fore

The centre of your universe

When you start caring for a loved one there is a lesson
you must quickly learn
If you do not then the frustration that builds will be
long term
At first I thought I could schedule things in nice little
time slots
But unfortunately no matter how I tried I found I could
not
It just leads to frustration and trying to hurry your
loved one along
It is the opposite of what is needed and is completely
wrong
You may try to fit things round your work and your
play
But very soon you will learn it does not work that way
In days of old people thought the sun revolved round
the earth
They were of course wrong and you will also find you
are no longer the centre of your universe
Accept the way things are and make changes in your
life
Lean in to love and give your loved one their best life
The only control you will have is over the changes you
choose to make
Putting your loved one at the centre is the best decision
you can take

Working from that starting point will make things
easier it is true
Then build your life around this including making time
for you
Focus then on making the journey for your loved one
the best you can do

Faith, Hope and Love

When you accompany a loved one on their dementia
journey
It strikes me that you need faith in many ways

You need faith in the doctors and nurses who are well
trained in what they do
That doesn't mean you should never question them as
nobody knows your loved one better than you.
Medication is needed when it will do good but no harm
But sometimes a "fiblet" can be better than a tablet to
keep your loved one calm

You need faith in your loved one that they are doing
their best
They are not trying to make the journey a trial or a test
Nobody can imagine just what they are going through
And it is never their intention to make things difficult
for you

You need faith in your family and friends supporting
you
You will often need to lean on them when you don't
know quite what to do
They may sometime say things that you may not want
to hear

But it is only because they have your interests at heart
and love you dear

You need faith in yourself that you too are doing your
best
And sometimes you need and are entitled to take a rest
Don't be too hard on yourself when it is a difficult time
You may get things wrong sometimes but will get them
right next time
Trying to make each day the best it can be for your
loved one is what you try to do
And nobody can ask any more of you

You need faith in God above that he will look after you
and your loved one too
Only God knows what's round the corner and what's
in front of you
Never try to work it out or ask why me or why us it is a
logic of which we are not capable
Simply trust that you will not have to cope with any
more than you are able
Looking back on your journey you may find only one
footprint in the sand
Where God was carrying you both I am sure you
understand

Never give up hope and each day is a new day
And always remember love will see you through most
things you have to do
The love you show your loved one, love for God and
love for you

Dementia – Hidden gifts

Family relationships have a vital part to play in easing the dementia journey. When looking at what people have written on different family relationships what strikes me most is both the strength and the beauty of the relationships. Despite the difficult circumstances both parties can gain much from the relationship. Thankfully our family relationship has always been very good but even in situations where the relationship in the past hasn't always been as good as it might have been it is possible for relationships to change and to strengthen. I tend to think that despite the terrible journey that is dementia, it leaves hidden gifts for all.

The Hidden Gifts of Dementia

When dementia comes calling it can be hard for the
family
It brings with it worry, pain and heartache to name just
three
 It comes with challenging behaviours, that can be
difficult to understand
And sometimes all you can do, is hold your loved one's
hand
But in amongst the pain, and rather than feeling sad
Take a step back sometimes, and try to look very hard
Like a light shining in the darkness you'll find
The Hidden Gifts of Dementia, and the Magic of the
Mind.

With Dad's Dementia emotions come to the fore
Uninhibited by conventions they sometimes let him
soar
He sings and often he dances with joy unconfined
Music often the key, to the Magic of the Mind

Dad has faith in all the family, and hope for them all
But the greatest of his emotions, is love for one and all
Dad forever tells us he loves us, and wishes God's
blessings upon us
With loving hugs and kisses, never far from us
They come always, with a loving smile

Which takes away the heartache, if only for a while
There is gentleness and warmth, in private moments
too
Alongside pearls of wisdom, to forget them would
never do
So always look hard dear friend and you will find
Hidden deep inside, the Magic of the Mind

So forget the challenging behaviours they belong to
Dementia and not to Dad
Always take a step back and never let yourself feel sad
Value the tender moments, pearls of wisdom, humour
and the smiles
A collective sense of healing they'll bring and be with
you all the while

To care for those who cared for us is a great gift and
honour to appreciate
Though it may not always feel so it is a Hidden Gift so
great
So in amongst the difficult days of which there will be
many from the start
Hang on to the Hidden Gifts and Blessings and always
treasure them in your heart

Family

The journey we are on with Dad is very much a family affair with both Mum and Dad at the centre and with myself, my sister Donna and her family, and my brother Steven and his family. The collection of poems in this section reflects this.

Dear Mum

Dear Mum you struggle to walk, even with sticks and
wheels to hold
Legs and feet refusing to do as they are told
Trapped inside, confined to a chair
Not able to go out, it doesn't seem fair

Dear Mum, your body is more frail than it used to be
Your shoulders are hunched as we can all see
Your hand sometimes trembles and your grip is not the
same
While arthritis in your back gives you so much pain

Dear Mum you find it so difficult to sleep at night
You go to bed hoping for the best but an hour or so
later you are back in the light
A hot drink and a chat then a sleep in the armchair
Or back to the bedroom pushed in the wheelchair

Dear Mum you love Dad oh so dearly, but on top of it
all
It made things more difficult when, for Dad, Dementia
came to call
Dad forever tells you he loves you and holds your hand
But a lot of the time he doesn't recognise you and can't
understand

Dear Mum you never complain
No matter how much you are in pain
You listen and chat and are here for us all
Your smile lights up the room and always cheers one
and all

Blessings

One cold winter some twenty-five plus years ago
My family all caught the cold and sore throat that was
on the go
The sore throat I remember was particularly bad
For Mum it was the worst she'd ever had
For us the cold and sore throat passed
For Mum it just seemed to last
After three sets of antibiotics it was still no better
So it was off to the hospital with a referral letter

On coming home from work one day, my Mum and
Dad were waiting
To give me some news that was quite heart breaking
The Doctors at the hospital had done their testing
Sadly they had found it was Cancer from which Mum
was suffering
My Mum and Dad were calm, no doubt had shed some
tears when they came home
For me the tears started to flow and to compose myself
I needed a short moment on my own
The journey it was starting then
The aim for Doctors and us all to get Mum well again

The treatment prescribed was courses of chemotherapy
Followed later by accompanying radiotherapy
It meant daily visits to hospitals a good few miles away

That seemed to go on for what felt like an eternity
These included the Beatsons in Glasgow which is well
known
As a specialist in cancer treatment of some renown
Some of the hospitals were quite run down physically
But the staff were excellent the Doctors especially

The journey it was hard for Mum
The travelling, the stress and the treatment that was to
come
Meant sickness, hair falling out, and being physically
very ill
Yet the programme of treatment gave little time to sit
still
My Mum she remained positive all the way
Fighting hard step by step every single day
My Dad accompanied Mum throughout the journey
Remaining strong, he was Mum's rock, hiding his pain,
along the way
That pain was shared by my sister, my brother and
myself,
 pain which we still remember to this day

I prayed to the Lord, to Our Lady and to Pope John
Paul too
I went to Church on Sundays and some week days as
well
Please oh please let my Mum get well.

My prayers they were answered, a blessing on our
family
The doctors they used their gifts to get Mum back
healthy

I prayed again, thank you Lord, Our Lady and Pope
John Paul
For granting this blessing upon us all

As a family we remain thankful that Mum is still with
us today
Walking again together this time on Dad's difficult
journey

Please Let Me Sleep

Why oh why do I find it so difficult to sleep at night
I go to bed hoping for the best but a few hours later I
am back in the light
A hot drink and a chat then stay in the armchair
Or back to the bedroom pushed in the wheelchair

I have tried counting people, I have tried counting
sheep
But no matter what I count, I still can't fall asleep
Hot milky drinks, cold drinks, no drinks at all
I have tried tips from everyone but asleep I can't fall

I have changed my mattress as it was quite old
My room is neither too hot nor is it too cold
I have tried everything that I have been told
But still sleep hasn't taken hold

A tablet from the doctor, then he increased it to two
Together with a kind word, I hope this will help you
That gave me some hope it is certainly true
But still a good sleep remains well overdue

I am at the end of my tether and don't know what's
keeping me from sleep
I am old and tired and just want to weep
Please oh please let me get a good night's sleep

Thank you

Many years ago when in the first job I obtained
A very perceptive boss described me as very self
contained
For very many people the perception of an accountant
that is often so
Is the person whose job it is to always just say no
You may recognise these traits as being with me still
If I can do it myself then indeed I will
I like to do things myself and that's what I will arrange
I can be very defensive and resistant to change
The result is I will often say no to help no matter where
it is from
Put my head down keep on working and just carry on

It doesn't mean I don't listen
It doesn't mean I don't consider other opinions
It doesn't mean I don't need help when it is appropriate
It doesn't mean the offers and the support I don't
appreciate

So thank you Dear Sister for the daily doses of loving
therapy in our telephone calls
For pushing me to change things when you thought it
needed to be so
Despite my resistance and tendency to say no

Thank you for your FaceTimes , message deliveries and
for the songs
And despite your daily pain, for coming along

So thank you Dear Brother for the kind and friendly
words and for being around
For the things I can't do by myself and lending a
helping hand
For the middle of night lifts and how you understand
Thank you for the concerts, solos and duets
And thank you also just as much for the tea time visits

Without you both I couldn't cope and want to say
thank you and I do appreciate it
We support each other as families should just as we
have been taught it
We share the love we share the guilt for things we've
done and things we've not
When we can be here and when we cannot
For just now and for future times we must always
remember
The love Mum and Dad have given us and that's how
we should support each other

Donna   **Steven**

The Covid Pandemic

The Covid Pandemic has brought pain, hardship and loss to many and probably no one living through it has been unaffected. The two poems below reflect on this first of all from the wider dementia community perspective and then at a specific and more practical level in terms of our family.

The Pandemic

The Covid Pandemic created difficulties for all
For many, sadly, it was their final call

For residents in care homes they became like prisoners
there in
No visitors or hugs from loved ones as well as the risk
of Covid lurking within
For those not able to visit and reduced to FaceTime or a
Zoom call
Hardly a visit, the stress unbearable for all
For those living at home, they were locked down and
imprisoned too
Not able to go out and visit, or for families to come to
you

Some care home staff went above and beyond, moving
in to the homes
Leaving their own families temporarily to fend for
themselves alone
Seeking to protect those they looked after, a selfless
thing to do
Examples like so many who led by example to get us
through

For those with dementia and their loved ones wherever
they lived

The problems the pandemic created
They simply cannot be overstated
For everyone the pandemic and its effects were difficult
to comprehend
For those with dementia, many simply could not
understand
Why were they getting no visits?
What has happened to their children, husband, wife?
Do they not love them any more?
This is no kind of life
Why can't we go out?
Why do I need to get jabs in my arm?
For the loved ones doing the caring, already
overworked and stressed
The pandemic meant additional challenges, and even
less rest
No day centres to rely on or music groups at all
More challenging behaviours and less support on
which to call

The long term effects are not yet measurable, only time
will tell
Just how bad it was for those with dementia and their
loved ones as well

Lockdown

The pandemic meant we locked down at home, my
Mum, my Dad and me
This meant a lot of changes for us some big some small
as you will see

We went for online shopping with groceries left outside
But for Dad who has dementia this didn't seem quite
right
For Dad and I did the shopping, Mum not fit to go
To the supermarket we'd always go with their row
upon row upon row
Dad enjoyed the drive in the car and helping with the
shopping
He'd push the trolley helping me and often to strangers
he'd start talking
Sometimes we'd meet people that my Dad knew or
worked with in the past
Dad didn't always remember who they were but still
enjoyed the chats
By the time we got home he'd not be able to tell Mum
who we'd met, the memory didn't last
When we reached the checkouts the operators knew us
too
My Dad would often ask them "to reduce the prices
and I'll sing a song for you"

Dad enjoyed the shopping trips, they helped break the day even when we went quite late
Unfortunately they had to stop the risks for Mum and Dad too great

Lockdown meant no visits from family or friends
This was the toughest thing with which we had to contend
Being at home with no visitors was bound to lead to "cabin fever"
Which with dementia can often lead to "challenging behaviours"
Stress caused by lockdown, dementia multiplying that stress as well
That meant a difficult time for all in this situation as you could probably tell

Visits they were replaced by FaceTime calls it was good to see the family
My Dad he likes to sing and for everyone else to join in happily
The calls they quickly turned into concerts and sing songs
Everyone had to be armed with a song and others had to sing along
Some chat at the start just to catch up was ok
But a little less conversation a lot more singing please was Dad's preferred way
The calls they did help us, my Dad particularly
They certainly helped to take some stress away often at the end of a difficult day

Afternoons out that we usually enjoyed they had to stop
A drive and a walk, finishing at a café for tea unfortunately went the same way as the shop
We had to find a new place to walk where there weren't many people around
This we eventually did in a forest nearby where the birds singing was the only sound
This sometimes changed when Dad wanted to sing and we'd march up and down singing aloud
There was nobody to see
Which given my singing certainly suited me
When we were done, it was back home to Mum, and a cuppa and a scone for all three

Vaccinate, Vaccinate, Vaccinate is the way out of this the government did say
Little did they know the challenge this sent our way
In times gone by, Dad would happily give blood and needles no problem for him
Unfortunately now someone jabbing his arm he thinks is deliberately doing him harm
Despite hearing of Covid every day on the news
My Dad doesn't understand or forgets and when I explain gets even more confused
The Covid booster and flu jag together was the worst, one on its own bad enough you see
The Nurse came on her own and jabbed both my Mum and me but Dad would have none of it, she wasn't doing three
Favourite music videos, numbing cream and sedative we'd try
No real help I don't know why

Two Nurses came back another day
Strength in numbers and extra distraction was to be the
way
The flu jab went in, some success, but Dad wasn't
happy at all
Enough is enough was the call
Having to put Dad through it again,
We did wonder should we and if so when
A different nurse she came on her own
Experienced working with dementia patients in care
homes
She had my Dad smiling and jabbed him as well
Then calmed him down, she was experienced you
could tell
A sigh of relief from Mum and me
Time to put the kettle on for tea

The Government has now all but eased all restrictions,
yet Covid rates are still sky high
I can't help but wonder what happens now to the
vulnerable and why?

Dementia – The Big Picture

The poems in this section are my thoughts and reflections on dementia in general and particular issues related to it as opposed to just the journey my family is on.

Dementia

My Dad has dementia and we live alongside it every day
It is difficult for Dad and for family
So I have penned these few words to hopefully help in some small way
There is no vaccination but things you can still do, so please for your sake, read them carefully

Dementia is increasing
50 Million people worldwide are living with dementia today
150 million are projected to be living with dementia by two thousand and fifty
Multiply that again by family members who are living alongside dementia every day
What more then do I really need to say!

Dementia can come early
Dementia can come late
Dementia can be genetic but most often is not
Dementia affects men but is also more prevalent in women
Dementia doesn't discriminate by race
Dementia doesn't discriminate by location

Dementia comes like a superpower to take over the mind
Dementia makes you forget things in many different ways
Dementia makes us forget little things just to start with
Dementia makes us forget what we just said
Dementia makes us forget where we are
Dementia makes us forget the way home
Dementia makes us forget where rooms in our home are
Dementia makes us forget names of loved ones
Dementia makes us forget things that happened yesterday
Dementia makes us forget things that happened five minutes ago

Dementia makes it difficult for you to sometimes understand
Dementia means you often need a helping hand
Dementia can make you behave so very differently
Dementia make no mistake affects the whole family
Dementia can affect your vision and what you actually see
You never know just how challenging living with dementia can be

The advice from me to you is try and avoid dementia in any way you can
Reduce your risk by not smoking or drinking alcohol more than you should
Make sure you maintain a healthy weight and eat a balanced diet when it comes to food
Take regular exercise and look after your heart

Be careful of diabetes and high blood pressure as a start
Try and stay socially active and stimulate your brain
If you have hearing loss make sure you get a hearing aid as you'll be sure to gain
Avoid isolation and depression and try and keep your mood high
Ask for help if you need it, there are plenty standing by
Make sure you get good rest and good sleep too
It really will help and be good for you
These things are not rocket science and you've probably heard them before
But unless you want to be one of the 150 Million please do heed them I implore

The Dementia Race

Dementia is running as fast as it can
Infecting many people all over the land
Unless we keep up where will it end
50M people in the world already have it today
150M projected to have it by two thousand and fifty

We too must run just to keep up with it
To find a cure and to prevent it
This needs funds and the best researchers
As well as changing our lifestyle behaviours

People that know and people that care
Do so much with love to get us there
They run to beat dementia
They swim to beat dementia
They cycle to beat dementia
And so much beside
But oh how we need so much more
From governments around the world to not let the
numbers soar

They say a pandemic dementia it is not
But 150Million people multiplied by family members is
still an awful lot!
They say that Dementia is not contagious, but try
asking the family

Living with dementia and living alongside has pain for
all to see
I say treat it as if a pandemic then more action there
would be
If we do not then we are all guilty
Spend the money and reduce the long term cost is what
we must do
That the accountants would get their long term rate of
return would undoubtedly be true
It just needs global leaders with vision all across the
world
Then Dementia we will out run you in the race around
the world

Head the Ball

When we were kids we'd be football mad
When the sun was out we'd have a kickabout and so
much fun we had
Other football games as well we chose
Such as 'headers' in the close
Head Head Head Head Head with a ball too big for us
First to five the winner, to the damage we're oblivious

When we were a bit older we'd play for football teams
Cross and head, cross and head, the trainer would drill
into us till we heard it in our dreams
Or head it hard and clear they told defenders, get the
ball away from the other teams
Head Head Head Head Head with a ball in those days
still very heavy for us
Score a goal and win the match, to the damage we're
oblivious

Later still some 'lucky' ones signed up to the
professional ranks
Football drills they'd do each day honing their talent
and their skills
Heading drills a priority for centre forwards and centre
halfs
They each must win the ball in the air and head it hard
and that is no laugh

Head Head Head Head Head every day, who's as good as us?
Win the cup or win the league, to the damage we're oblivious

Now today it's sad to say
Many of those who had such skill in their day
Are battling hard to win in a very different way
Head Head Head Head Head they were oblivious every day
Was also inviting Dementia to come along and to stay
With them and with their family

Football mad we all still are but lessons we need to learn
Keep the ball on the ground shouts the trainer, the motto for the new season
That's how this Dementia team can easily be beaten
And that has to be the best reason

For Governments, Footballing Authorities, Coaches, Players and Parents
The damage from dementia is something of which we are now all very much aware
And the time has come to show how just how much you care
Use your Head Head Head Head Head in different ways as we are no longer oblivious
Help those who suffer and their families from world cup winners to lower league players
They need us one and all
But most of all protect our children and players of the future from the time they first pick up a ball

Rover Helps You Remember

I received an e-mail today
My monthly update from those clever people at
Alzheimers Research UK
It reported a study in the US
Which claimed long term pet ownership results in
memory decline being less
More research is required it is true
But it sounds like the calming effect and
companionship is not only good for you
 It helps your memory too

Music Therapeutic

Most people enjoy listening to music
But it is not just fun it is therapeutic
For those with dementia even more so
A sing along always on the go

"Quando Quando Quando"
Sang 79 year old Ted who has dementia, and his son
Simon
Their car pool karaoke soon became an internet
sensation

80 year old dementia sufferer Paul
Composed music from four notes that's all
He recorded a single with the BBC Philharmonic and
released it to the nation
A clip of it went viral, another internet sensation

I know from my own experience with my Dad
The powerful effect music has had
It helps to calm Dad when he is upset
His favourite songs and videos available on the internet
He loves to sing on his own, even more so when
everyone sings along
Despite his problems with memory he still remembers
the words to every song

Music for Dementia and the Dementia choir too
Have provided proof that if you have dementia how
music and song can help you
Singing groups have sprung up in many locations
across the land
Often organised by Alzheimers Society and Alzheimers
Scotland
Wonderful charities that are always there to lend
families a helping hand
The power of music in helping with dementia and
relieving much stress
Is now so convincing it should be prescribed on the
NHS

Everyone Has a Poem

It is often said that everyone has a book in them. Whether or not that is true I do believe it is certainly true that everyone has a poem in them.

It doesn't matter whether you have never written a poem before, I hadn't until recently. It also doesn't matter what your writing skills are as poems are often about the spoken word and can be written as they are spoken.

I would encourage everyone therefore to take some time out and sit down and write or speak a poem. You may well find it therapeutic and it may also give you a sense of satisfaction when it is done. It may well let you express your feelings in a way you can't necessarily do any other way.

I believe that poetry has a great deal to offer those living with dementia and their families and caregivers. Both in terms of expressing their creativity and indeed in reading and sharing it.

As you will know, all my royalties from this book go to Alzheimers Research UK and I have received no payment for writing the book.

As a follow on project I am looking to compile another book of poems. I would like anyone who wishes, to send me a poem, or poems, particularly those in the Dementia community. It doesn't need to be about dementia and can be about anything as there is still life outside dementia and the creativity of people with dementia and their families, caregivers and those involved with dementia research, support and charities is great.

Depending on the volume of poems I will publish a quarterly collection of some of the poems and send them out to all subscribers for a small subscription and publish a poetry book annually with a lot more of the poems. Again all royalties will go to dementia charities and all poems published will have full accreditation to their authors in the quarterly collection and annual book.

The hope is that as more and more people find confidence and enjoyment in writing poems and write them more regularly and the publications can become an ongoing thing and raise regular much needed funds for dementia charities.

Please e-mail all poems to:

Pat@Poemsfordementia.com

Website: www.poemsfordementia.com

All poems must be your own work as we want to respect others' privacy and not infringe copyright. By submitting a poem you are agreeing you are the author and you are giving permission for us to publish it as described above.

Go on, give it a go, you know you have it in you! □

Finally, I really hope that you have found the book helpful and enjoyed reading some of the poems. It would be great if you could leave a review on Amazon which would help encourage others to read it and raise additional funds for Alzheimers Research.

Thank you

Pat

About the Author

Pat McTaggart is a qualified accountant and spent 25+ years as a Finance Director/CFO and most recently joint CEO within the IT and Software sectors.
He has a strong interest in social enterprise and the charitable sectors and sat on the Board of two charities. Over the last three years Pat has been full time carer to his Mum and Dad living with them in their home in Scotland.

He can be contacted at:

pat@poemsfordementia.com
Twitter: @pat_mct
www.poemsfordementia.com

The Purple Angel

The Purple Angel shown below and appearing on the cover of this book in stamp form symbolises a guardian over those living with dementia, their families and friends and those helping to raise awareness of the disease. The Purple Angel Logo became embraced by individuals and organisations across the world and so the globe was added to show the impact and collaboration of this movement.

Now there is one symbol representing a global message
RAISING AWARENESS, HOPE AND
EMPOWERMENT
For all people living with dementia, their families and care partners.

Links to more information:

Purple Angel Project (alzheimersspeaks.com)
About Us – Purple Angels Global (purpleangel-global.com)

Printed in Great Britain
by Amazon

39156723R00066